# Benchmark ADVANCE
# Texts *for* English Language Development

BENCHMARK EDUCATION COMPANY

# Table of Contents

# Being a Good Community Member

## Essential Question

# Why do people get involved in their communities?

**My Language Objectives**

- Use categories
- Use verbs
- Use question marks
- Use proper nouns
- Use cause and effect signal words

**My Content Objectives**

- Build vocabulary related to community roles and responsibilities
- Understand the different ways people participate in their communities

3

# Hello, Community Garden!

**1**

Between the city buildings, one plot of land was a problem.

**2**

Some neighbors decided to turn the lot into a vegetable garden.

**3**

The plants grew big and healthy.

**4**

Soon there were delicious carrots, tomatoes, and beans for everyone to share.

**ThinkSpeakListen**

Tell the kinds of plants you see on this page.

# Katie's Crop

Katie wanted to help people. She had an idea.

She planted a tiny plant and took good care of it.

It grew into a huge cabbage! When she gave it away, it helped feed a lot of people.

Now other kids are growing food to give away, too.

**ThinkSpeakListen**
Retell how Katie helped people.
First Katie _____. Then _____. Next _____.

# Categories

## fruits

## vegetables

## people

## gardens

**Think**Speak**Listen**

Name some other garden plants.

# Kind Hearts Are Gardens

*by Henry Wadsworth Longfellow*

Kind hearts are the gardens,

gardens

Kind thoughts are the roots,

roots

Kind words are the flowers,

flowers

Kind deeds are the fruits.

fruits

**ThinkSpeakListen**

Add a new line to the poem.
Kind people are the _____.

# Safe to Go!

Garrett Morgan
was an inventor.

One day, he saw
a terrible accident.
A car collided with a
horse and carriage.

**ThinkSpeakListen**
Why do you think it is important to have rules for traffic?

8

In 1923, Morgan invented a signal that directed traffic safely.

Morgan's signal had signs that moved up and down like arms. Red meant "stop" and green meant "go."

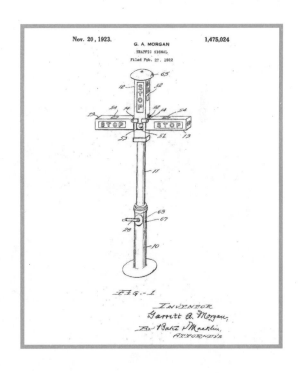

**ThinkSpeakListen**

How do traffic signals help to keep us safe?

# What Will Max Do?

**1**

Max really wants a snack, but he does not have enough money.

**2**

Is that a dollar on the floor? Max picks it up.

**3**

"Oh, no!" he hears Ana cry.

**4**

Max knows what to do.

**ThinkSpeakListen**
What do you think Max will do?

# Being a Responsible Citizen

Responsible citizens are fair and kind to other people. They **respect** other people.

**Responsible** citizens know that rules help keep us safe. Rules also help us get along with others.

**ThinkSpeakListen**
Tell what a responsible citizen does.

# Verbs

run

raise

shout

walk

**Think**Speak**Listen**

Tell which words describe an action that might break rules at school.

# Question Marks

Where could the class go on a field trip?

The class is going to the zoo.

How can she be responsible?

She can be fair and kind to others.

## ThinkSpeakListen

Which words ask a question? How can you tell?

13

# Being a Responsible Citizen

**Chapter 1**

Responsible Citizens
Are Honest

**Chapter 2**

Responsible Citizens
Respect Others

14

## Chapter 3

Responsible Citizens
Follow Rules

## Chapter 4

Responsible Citizens
Help Make Decisions

**ThinkSpeakListen**

Tell what each chapter is about.

# Jim Henson

Do you know who Jim Henson was?

Maybe not. But you know the puppets he created.

Kermit the Frog is one,

and Miss Piggy is another.

**ThinkSpeakListen**

Tell why someone would write about Jim Henson's life.

# Proper Nouns

Martin Luther King Jr.

Harriet Beecher Stowe

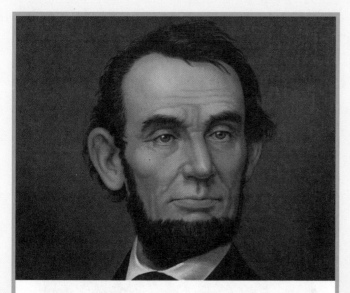

Abraham Lincoln

Sacajawea

**ThinkSpeakListen**

Talk about why these words are spelled with capital letters.

# People Who Made Contributions

## Chapter 1

Thousands of Cherokees learned to read and write in their own language because of Sequoyah.

## Chapter 2

Because of Frederick Douglass, many people worked together to free enslaved people.

## Chapter 3

Helen Keller helped improve life for people with special needs.

## Chapter 4

Because of Cesar Chavez, thousands of farm workers live better lives.

**ThinkSpeakListen**
Tell what each chapter is about.

# Pronouns

**She** aided those with special needs.

**He** worked to free the slaves.

**He** won rights for farm workers.

**They** all helped people.

**ThinkSpeakListen**

Tell which word stands for more than one person.

# Cause and Effect Signal Words

**Because** of Frederick Douglass, many people worked together to free enslaved people.

Helen Keller got very ill. **Afterward**, she could not see or hear.

Cherokees learned to read and write in their own language **because** of Sequoyah.

**ThinkSpeakListen**

Find the words that say one thing caused another.

# Many Kinds of Characters

## Essential Question

## How do we learn about people?

**My Language Objectives**

- Use noun and verb agreement
- Use nouns
- Use sound words
- Use sequence signal words
- Use comparison words

**My Content Objectives**

- Build vocabulary related to literary characters
- Understand how folktales and fairy tales develop characters

# The Ant and the Grasshopper

**①**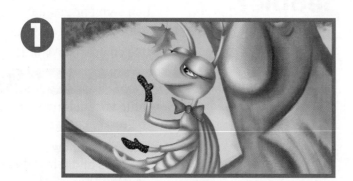

All summer, the lazy grasshopper laughed at the responsible, hardworking ant.

**②**

But the ant kept working and replied, "I'm preparing for winter, and so should you!"

**③**

Soon summer turned to fall, and fall became winter.

Now the grasshopper was weak with hunger!

**④**

"Dear friend, I need some food!" he demanded.

"I'm sorry, but there isn't enough for both of us," explained the ant.

**ThinkSpeakListen**
Retell the story.
First _____. Then _____. Next _____. Last _____.

24

# A Pet for Meg

Meg wanted a pet. Dad said, "Let's go to the shelter!"

They looked at lots of cute pets. Then Meg saw Pixie. Her fur was a mess and her tongue stuck out!

"Who would take *this* dog?" asked Dad.

"I will!" said Meg. And she did!

**ThinkSpeakListen**

Pretend you are Meg and tell what you like about Pixie.

# Noun and Verb Agreement

The puppy eats.

The puppies eat.

The ant crawls.

The ants crawl.

**Think Speak Listen**

Tell what a grasshopper does.

# Read to Me

*by Jane Yolen*

Read to me riddles
and read to me rhymes,

Read to me stories
of magical times.

Read to me tales
about castles and kings,

Read to me stories
of fabulous things.

Read to me pirates,
and read to me knights,

read to me dragons
and dragon-back flights.

**ThinkSpeakListen**

Add something new to read about.
Read to me tales about _____ and _____.

27

# Little Red Riding Hood

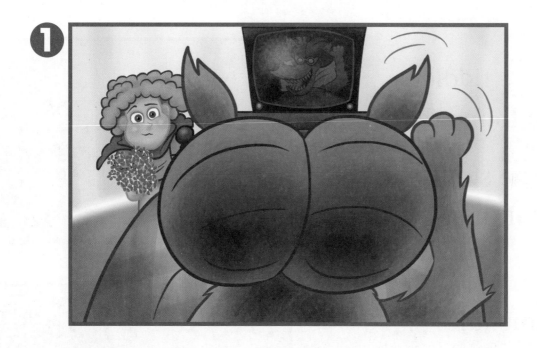

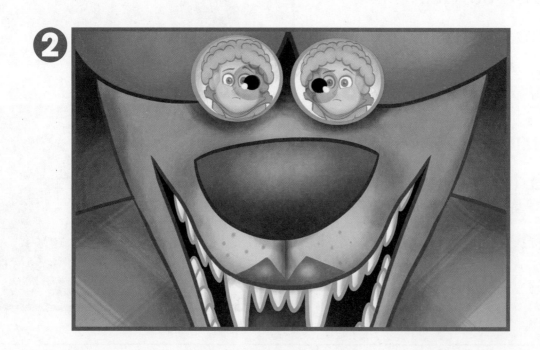

**3**

**4**

**Think Speak Listen**

Retell the story.

# The Tortoise and the Hare

Hare bragged about how fast he could run. He teased Tortoise for being slow.

One day Tortoise said, "Let's race!" Hare took off!

He bragged, "I'll take a nap and still win!"

Tortoise passed Hare and kept going—slow and steady. Tortoise won! Hare never bragged again.

**ThinkSpeakListen**

Tell how Tortoise won.

# The Princess and the Pea

Once upon a time, there was a prince who wanted to marry a princess.

The prince traveled all over the world to find his true princess, but there was always something not quite right.

One evening there was a terrible storm.

Someone knocked at the town gate. The prince himself went to open it.

**ThinkSpeakListen**
Who do you think is at the door?

# Nouns

## Royalty

king

prince

princess

knight

**ThinkSpeakListen**

Tell which of these is the most powerful.

# Sound Words

crashed

howled

**Think**Speak**Listen**
Tell some other sound words.

# The Princess and the Pea

**1**

**2**

**3**

**4**

**5**

**6**

**7**

**8**

# Chums

*by Arthur Guiterman*

He sits and begs, he gives
a paw.

And he belongs to me.

He follows everywhere I go,

And even when I swim.

I laugh because he thinks,
you know,

That I belong to him.

**ThinkSpeakListen**
Say the poem aloud. Listen for the rhyming words.

# Sequence Signal Words

**First** the old woman got some flour and sugar.

**Next** she got a bowl and a spoon and a cup.

**Then** she made a Gingerbread Man.

**ThinkSpeakListen**

Say what the old woman will do next.

# The Gingerbread Man

**Out** jumped the
Gingerbread Man.

As he ran, he called,

**Run, run, as fast as
you can.**

**You can't catch me,**

**I'm the Gingerbread Man.**

The little old man and
woman, the boy and the
girl, the dog and the cat,
all ran after him.

Until suddenly, he came to
a wide river.

Then along came a fox.
"Don't worry," he said. "I'll
carry you over the river."

SNIP

SNAP!

The fox gobbled up the
Gingerbread Man in one bite.

**ThinkSpeakListen**
Tell what happens in each scene.

39

# Nouns

## Parts of the Body

head

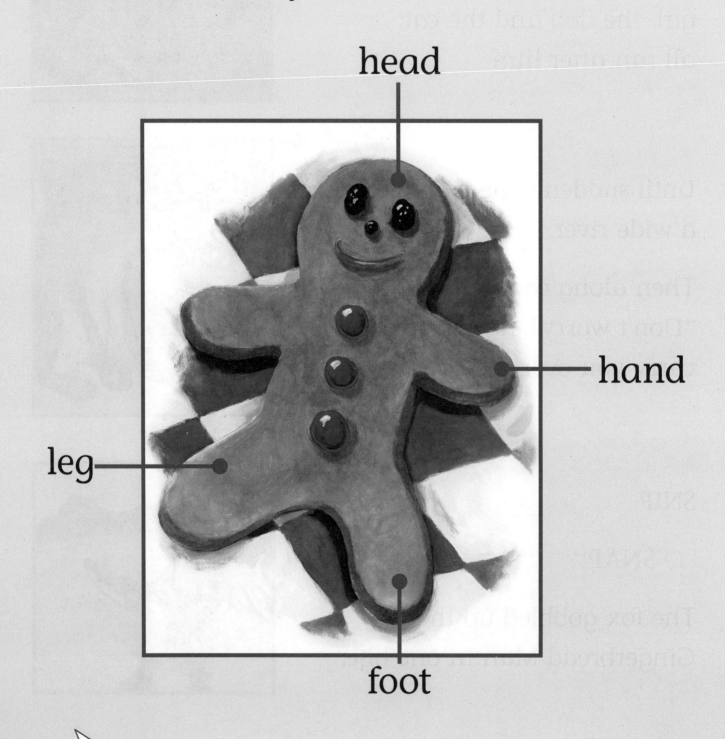

hand

leg

foot

**ThinkSpeakListen**

Tell other parts of your body on your hands, feet, and head.

# Comparison Words

The Gingerbread Man ran **fast**.

Then he ran even **faster**.

The cat came **close**.

The fox came even **closer**.

**ThinkSpeakListen**

Say why the Gingerbread Man ran fast and then faster.

41

# Plants and Animals
# Grow and Change

**1**

**The Life Cycle**

**3**

pupa

**4**

butterfly

# Why do living things change?

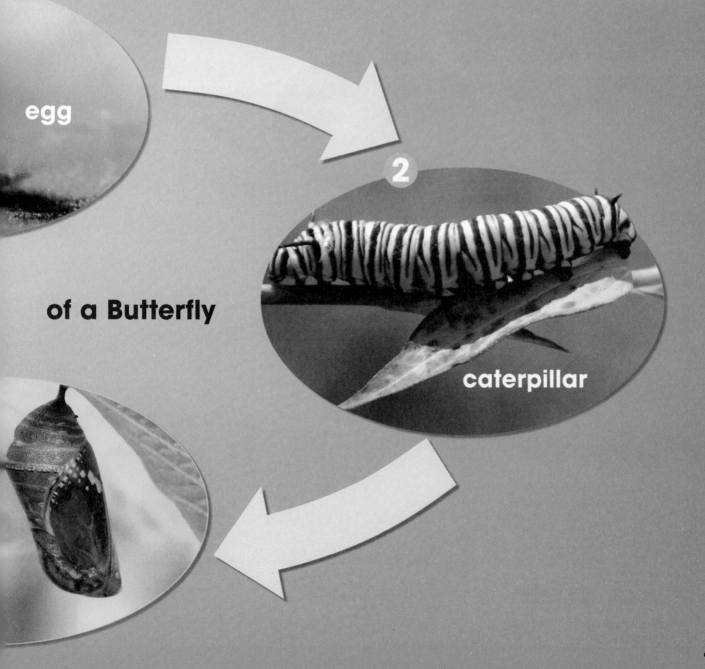

egg

of a Butterfly

2

caterpillar

# The Amazing Life Cycle of a Frog

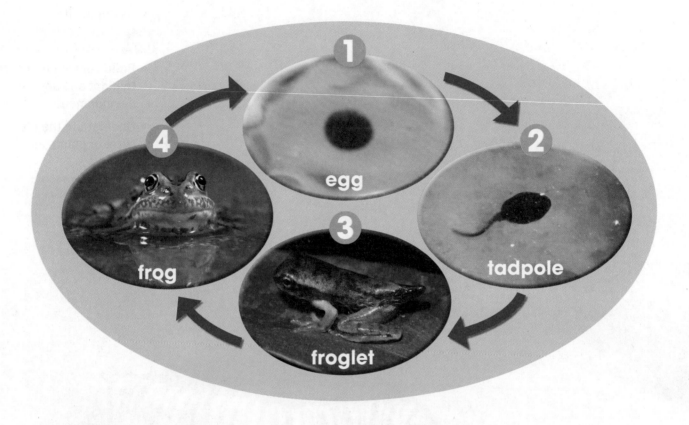

First, a female frog lays eggs in water.

Then the tadpole hatches from the egg.

Next, the tadpole grows. It's a froglet.

At last, the froglet is an adult frog.

**ThinkSpeakListen**

Act out the steps in order.

# The Amazing Butterfly

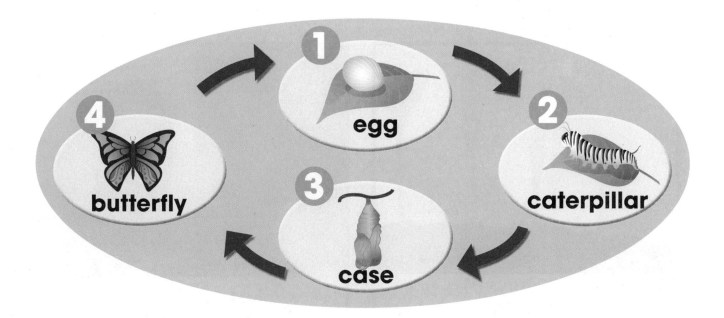

First a butterfly laid a tiny egg on a leaf.

Then the egg hatched. A little caterpillar crawled out. The caterpillar ate and ate.

Next it made itself a case. The caterpillar changed inside the case.

At last, out came a butterfly!

**ThinkSpeakListen**
Retell the steps.
First _____. Then _____. Next _____.

# Verbs

grow

change

hatch

crawl

**ThinkSpeakListen**

Say what the baby is doing.

# Caterpillar

*by Christina Rossetti*

Brown and furry

Caterpillar in a hurry,

Take your walk

To the shady leaf, or stalk

**ThinkSpeakListen**

Tell about things that are furry.
Tell about things that are brown.

47

# The Fox and the Robin

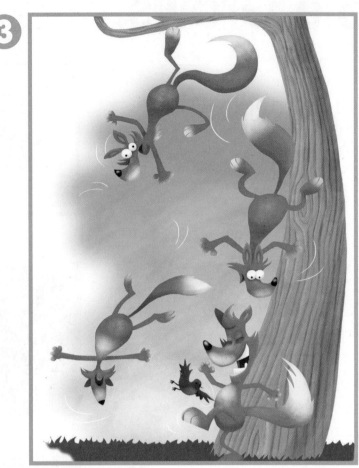

## ThinkSpeakListen

Retell the story.

# An Apple Grows

In the center of an apple, there are seeds.

Those seeds can grow into apple trees.

Flowers bloom on apple trees every spring.

In the spot where each flower was, an apple starts to grow.

**ThinkSpeakListen**

Retell the life cycle of an apple.

# An Oak Tree Has a Life Cycle

**Chapter 1**

At first, a fully grown oak tree drops **seeds**. These seeds are acorns.

**Chapter 2**

A few months after the acorn falls, **roots** begin to grow.

Next, a **stem** grows from the acorn.

At last, the stem becomes a thick, strong **trunk**.

# Noun and Verb Agreement

The  grows.

acorn

The  grow.

acorns

The  grows.

tree

The  grow.

trees

**ThinkSpeakListen**

Tell what happens to one seed.
Tell what happens to many seeds.

# Prepositions

seed

## The seeds are **in** the apple.

## The acorn is **on** the ground.

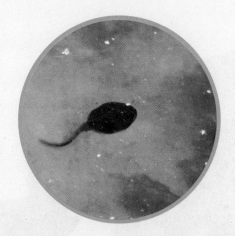

## The tadpole is **in** the water.

## The egg is **on** the leaf.

**ThinkSpeakListen**

Say each thing you see in the pictures. Then say where it is.
Use the words **in** and **on**.

53

# An Oak Tree Has a Life Cycle

1 acorns

4 oak tree

② roots

③ stem and leaves

**Think**Speak**Listen**
Retell the life cycle.

# Welcome, Ducklings!

Ducklings can walk when they are just one day old.

They know how to swim, too.

The mother duck keeps her ducklings together, so they will be safe.

When ducklings are two months old, they are able to fly.

**ThinkSpeakListen**
Act out what ducks can do.

56

# Nouns and Verbs

The  can  .

duck · fly

The  can  .

duckling · swim

Can the   ?

duckling · fly

Can the   ?

duck · swim

**ThinkSpeakListen**

Tell what ducks can do.

# The Ugly Duckling

Out popped a big gray duckling.

"Who are **you**?" said the mother duck.

"Go away! Go away! You're **ugly**," chirped the five yellow ducklings.

The ugly duckling grew very sad. "No one wants me," he said.

So he swam sadly off down the river.

**5**

The duckling hid among the reeds. He was cold and hungry, and all alone.

**6**

After a long time, the ice began to melt. And the birds began to sing.

**7**

Slowly the duckling ruffled his feathers.

**8**

The ugly duckling was **not** an ugly duckling any more.

## ThinkSpeakListen

Tell what happens in each scene.

59

# Color Words

The  is .

duckling    yellow

The  is  .

fox    orange

The  is .

frog    green

The  is  .

butterfly    blue

**ThinkSpeakListen**

Tell about colors you see.

# Opposites

happy

sad

cold

hot

big

little

**ThinkSpeakListen**

Say two things about the girls in the pictures.

# Stories Have a Narrator

Once upon a time, there was a cat....

## Essential Question

## How do people create stories?

**My Language Objectives**

- Use verbs
- Use proper nouns
- Use animal sounds
- Use rhyming words
- Use describing words
- Use prepositions

**My Content Objectives**

- Build vocabulary related to the narration of stories
- Understand the process by which people create stories

# The City Mouse and the Country Mouse

**1** I visited my dear cousin, Kate, who lives in the country. Her home was inside a plain, old log.

**2** At night, it was so quiet I couldn't sleep! Country life was boring.

**3** I visited my cousin, Clyde, who lives in a fancy house in the city. There were breads, cheeses, and fruit on the table.

**4** As we began eating, two huge cats appeared! I headed home, where it's peaceful!

**ThinkSpeakListen**
Retell the story.
First _____. Then _____. Next _____. Last _____.

64

# Home Sweet Home

Do you know the yellow house?

I live there. Maybe you have seen me napping on the step.

When my lady misses me, she calls, "Here, kitty!"

My name is not kitty! I will not come!

But now it's dark and cold, so I slink home.

"Tank!" she cries. "Where were you?"

It's good to be home.

**ThinkSpeakListen**
Say the words in the poem that are action words.

# Verbs

The  **naps**.

man

The  **slinks**.

cat

The 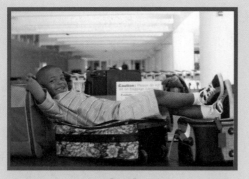 **visits**.

kid

**ThinkSpeakListen**
Tell what else a cat might do.

# Good Neighbors

*by May Justus*

A little old woman and
    a little old mouse

Live in the very same
    little old house.

She rocks in a corner,
He scampers in the wall,
And they never, never
    get in each other's
    way at all.

**ThinkSpeakListen**
Say what the old woman does.
Say what the mouse does.

# A Quiet Camping Trip

**③**

**④**

# A Big Fish?

"Come on, Jen," says Chip. "Let's go catch some fish!"

Something tugs on Chip's line!

Chip says, "I think I've caught a big one!"

It's not a big fish. It's a soggy, blue mitten!

**ThinkSpeakListen**
Why does Chip think he has a fish?

# Chicken Little

Chicken Little was walking through the woods when—*BONK*—an acorn fell on his head.

"GOODNESS GRACIOUS ME!" he cried. "The sky is falling! I must go and tell the king!"

He met Henny Penny basking in the sun. "Where are you going in such a hurry?" she clucked.

"I'm going to tell the king the sky is falling!" replied Chicken Little.

"I'll come with you," cried Henny Penny.

Before long, they came upon Ducky Lucky preening his feathers.

"Where are you going in such a hurry?" he quacked.

**ThinkSpeakListen**
What will Chicken Little say to Ducky Lucky? What will Ducky Lucky say?

# Proper Nouns

Chicken Little

Henny Penny

Ducky Lucky

**Think**Speak**Listen**

Tell what these names have in common.

# Animal Sounds

The  **clucked**.

hen

The  **quacked**.

duck

**ThinkSpeakListen**

What sounds do other animals make?

# Chicken Little

**Think**Speak**Listen**

Retell the story.

75

# I Had a Little Hen

I had a little hen, the prettiest
   ever seen,

She washed up the dishes and
   kept the house clean.

She went to the mill to fetch
   me some flour,

And brought it home in less
   than an hour.

She fetched me my mail,

She sat by the fire and told a
   fine tale!

**ThinkSpeakListen**
Could this happen in real life? Tell why or why not.

# Rhyming Words

Lily and I sifted two
   pounds of **flour**,

We had hot fresh cookies
   in under an **hour**.

Before Mom came home
   the kitchen was **clean**,

The most wonderful sight
   that ever was **seen**.

**ThinkSpeakListen**
Say two words that rhyme.

# The Fox and the Little Red Hen

Once upon a time, a little red hen lived by herself in a house near the woods.

On the other side of the woods, a crafty fox lived with his mother in a cave.

One morning, crafty Fox said to his mother, "Tonight I shall bring Little Red Hen home for supper."

Fox sneaked into her house. When Little Red Hen came inside, he pounced! Quickly Fox stuffed her into his bag.

As Fox walked back he decided to lie down and have a rest. Little Red Hen wriggled out of the bag. She rolled a big stone into the bag.

*SPLASH!* Into the pot fell the heavy stone.

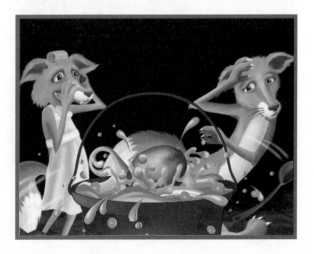

**ThinkSpeakListen**
Tell what happens in each scene.

# Describing Words

**crafty** fox

**big** bag

**heavy** stone

**fat** hen

**Think**Speak**Listen**

Tell another word that describes the red hen.

# Prepositions

She got **out** of the bag.

She put the rock **into** the bag.

The rock went **into** the water.

She was **out** of danger.

**Think**Speak**Listen**

Tell what the red hen did.

# Technology at Work

## Essential Question

# How can technology make a difference in our lives?

**My Language Objectives**

- Use technology words
- Use verb and noun agreement
- Use verbs
- Use rhyming words
- Use prepositions

**My Content Objectives**

- Build vocabulary related to using technology to accomplish tasks
- Understand the ways in which technology affects our lives

83

# Robots at Work

**1**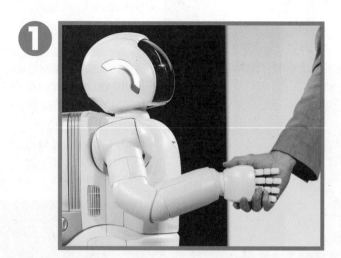

Many robots can move
around on wheels or legs.

**2**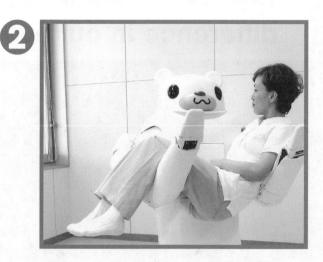

Some robots work
in hospitals.

**3**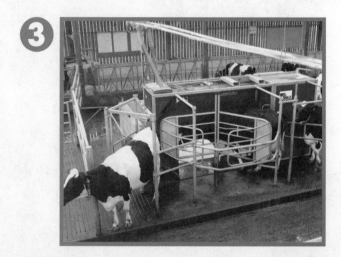

Cows walk into the robot
milker to be milked.

**4**

Can you imagine
having a robot serve
you in a restaurant?

**Think Speak Listen**
Tell about a job a robot can do.

# Carrier Pigeons

Did you know that some birds take messages to people? These birds are called carrier pigeons.

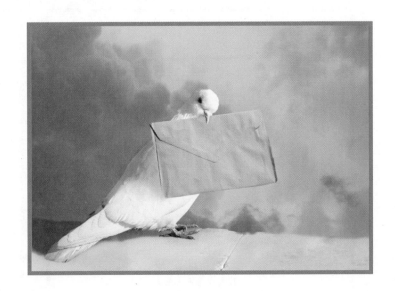

Many people used carrier pigeons long ago—before they had radios, phones, and computers.

**Think**Speak**Listen**
Tell what carrier pigeons do.

# Technology Words

## radio

## phone

## computer

## robot

**Think**Speak**Listen**

Tell what each type of technology does.

# Atom's Day Off

Data left for her job. Atom did all the chores in the house.

That day, Atom took a break. He lost track of time. *Oh, no!* There was no supper ready.

"It's OK," beeped Data. "I brought Bolt Burgers as a treat."

**ThinkSpeakListen**

How do you think Atom felt at the end of the story?

# What a Great Idea!

**3**

**4**

## ThinkSpeakListen
Retell the story.

# A Handy Machine

Some schools have a special way to make sure all the kids can get lunch. They don't need money or lunch cards.

They just have to scan their hands to pay for their lunches. It's like having a built-in code!

**ThinkSpeakListen**

What does it mean to scan your hand?

# Using Technology at Work

**Chapter 1**

Cartoonists make drawings come alive with the help of technology.

**Chapter 2**

The cockpit of an airplane is filled with technology.

**Chapter 3**

Mechanics use technology to help them identify what is wrong with a car.

**ThinkSpeakListen**

How does technology help the people pictured in the photographs?

# Technology Words

computer

tool

camera

**ThinkSpeakListen**

In what way are all of these things tools?

# Verb and Noun Agreement

Cartoonists **use** computers.

A cartoonist **uses** a computer.

Mechanics **use** tools.

A mechanic **uses** a tool.

**ThinkSpeakListen**

Tell what one person does with a camera.
Tell what many people do with cameras.

# Using Technology at Work

**Think**Speak**Listen**

Tell what each chapter is about.

# Unplug!

One group of people thought they were spending too much time looking at screens.

One day each week, they do not use cell phones or computers, or watch TV.

You can try it, too.

Go outside. Ride your bike, jump rope, or watch clouds drift by.

**ThinkSpeakListen**
What does the mark at the end of the title tell you?

96

# Verbs

## Unplugged Fun!

**Ride** your bike, **jump** rope, **play,** or **watch** the stars come out.

ride

jump

play

watch

**Think Speak Listen**

What can you do to unplug? I can _____.

# Technology Breakdown

Today, I'm at work with Dad.

Phones are ringing, e-mail is dinging, and screens everywhere are bing-bing-BINGING!

But for my dad, all that high-tech clatter does not matter.

Technology problems go all day long! But my dad always finds out what is wrong.

The boss says, "Thank you, you're the best! Now go on home and get some rest."

**ThinkSpeakListen**
Tell what happens in the story.
First _____. Then _____. Next _____. Last _____.

# Rhyming Words

When we go
driving the car
makes a **clatter**,

But to my mother
and me it does
not **matter**.

When I crossed
the line my time
was **best**,

After that I earned
some **rest**.

**ThinkSpeakListen**
Say some other rhyming words.

# Prepositions

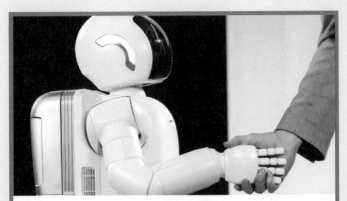

Many robots can move around **on** wheels or legs.

Some robots work **in** hospitals. One can lift patients.

Cows walk **into** the robot milker to be milked.

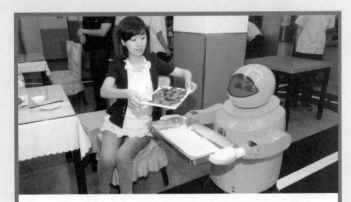

Imagine having a robot serve you **in** a restaurant?

**Think Speak Listen**

Tell other things robots can do.

# Stories Teach Many Lessons

# Essential Question

## What can we learn from a mistake?

**My Language Objectives**

- Use describing words
- Use nouns
- Use categories
- Use verbs
- Use plurals

**My Content Objectives**

- Build vocabulary related to the lessons that stories teach
- Understand how mistakes help us learn lessons

# The Boy Who Cried Wolf

**1**

Once there was a shepherd boy who looked after a flock of sheep. Sometimes the boy got very bored.

**2**

One day, the boy decided to play a trick and shouted, "Wolf! A wolf is chasing the sheep away!" The villagers came running to help.

**3**

A week later, he was bored again, and cried, "Wolf! Wolf!" Once more, the villagers came running.

**4**

Several days later, a wolf really came and chased the sheep away. "Wolf! Wolf!" the boy cried, but this time, no one came.

**ThinkSpeakListen**

How can you tell that the boy is yelling?

# Not So Scary

Pony lives on the farm. Pony likes the chickens.

Pony loves to dance with the funny goats, too.

What does Pony NOT like?

The large, scary cow.

One day, Pony goes outside to find Mama. Where can Mama be?

A gentle voice says, "Look over there, Pony."

It is the cow! She's not so scary after all.

**ThinkSpeakListen**
Why is Pony not scared anymore?

# Describing Words

large

scary

funny

angry

## ThinkSpeakListen

Tell a word that describes today's weather.

# The Strongest Things

*by Constance Andrea Keremes*

A tubby tugboat looks just like
    A toy to you and me.
But it is strong enough to pull
    A big ship out to sea.

A little ant no bigger than
    A spot upon the floor,
Can carry crumbs ten times his weight
    Quite easily through the door.

Some of the strongest things I see
    Are really very small.

**ThinkSpeakListen**
Say another word that could describe the size of an ant.

# The Ant and the Pigeon

**1**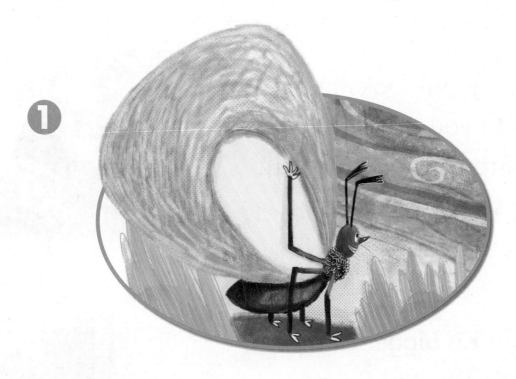

**2**

## ThinkSpeakListen
Retell the story.
First ____. Then ____. Next ____. Last ____.

# Pete Saves the Day

"Can I play?" Pete asked.

Gus said, "You are too small."

Pete sighed and sat to watch Gus bat.

CRACK! The ball rolled under a bush with huge, long thorns.

"These thorns are sharp, and my hand is too big," Gus said.

Pete said, "I can get it!" He put his small hand in. "Got it!"

**ThinkSpeakListen**
Tell which words from the story are describing words.

# Why Turtle's Shell Is Cracked

Turtle offered a trade with the other animals. If they brought him food, he would let them peer closely into his shiny shell.

As winter approached, food became scarce. The animals came up with a plan. The geese always flew south at this time. Perhaps they could take Turtle.

In no time at all, the geese were carrying Turtle through the sky. "LOOK AT ALL THE FOOD!" Turtle shouted joyfully.

Then...

**ThinkSpeakListen**
What do you think happens next?

# Nouns

turtle

bear

eagle

beaver

**ThinkSpeakListen**

What is another animal name?

# Categories

## Seasons

summer

fall

winter

spring

**ThinkSpeakListen**

Tell what season it is now. Tell what season is coming next.

113

# Why Turtle's Shell Is Cracked

## ThinkSpeakListen
Tell what each scene is about.

# Why Bear Has a Short Tail

One day Bear asked Fox how to catch many fish. Fox said, "Use your tail. Put it through the ice and fish will come and bite it."

So Bear made a hole in the ice and stuck his long, brown tail in the cold water.

Oh, no! His tail was frozen in the ice. He pulled until *pop!* Bear had only a short tail.

**Think** **Speak** **Listen**

What word in the story sounds like what it describes?

# Verbs

## Words That Describe Action

catch

bite

stick

pull

**ThinkSpeakListen**

Tell what action you do when you go up the stairs.

# Why Mosquitoes Buzz in People's Ears

Lion King pulled the sticks out of Iguana's ears. "Why did you not reply to Python's greeting this morning?" he asked.

"I did not hear him," said Iguana. "Mosquito was annoying me with tall tales, so I plugged up my ears."

"So," Lion King told the animals, "Iguana frightened Python, who scared Rabbit, then Rabbit startled Crow,

and Crow panicked Monkey, who knocked the branch that knocked the owlet.

And that is why Mother Owl is too sad to call the sun. It is Mosquito who is to blame."

Mosquito was punished.

To this very day, when his brothers and sisters buzz in people's ears, they ask, "**Zzzzzeeeeeee**?" Which means "Is everyone still angry with me?"

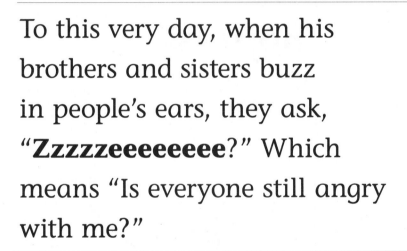

And to this day, mosquitoes always get the same answer: **THWACK!**

**Think**Speak**Listen**

Tell what happens in the story.
First _____. Then _____. Next _____. Last _____.

# Verbs

## Animal Movement

The python **slithered**.

The rabbit **hopped**.

The monkeys **swung**.

The iguana **scurried**.

**Think**Speak**Listen**

Think of an animal you like. What did that animal do?

# Plurals

tree

trees

egg

eggs

## ThinkSpeakListen

Name a kind of fruit. What would that fruit be called if you had two or more?

# Past, Present, and Future

past

present

## Essential Question

### Why is the past important?

**My Language Objectives**

- Use education words
- Use time words
- Use verb tenses
- Use proper nouns
- Use capital letters
- Use noun and verb agreement

**My Content Objectives**

- Build vocabulary related to the past, present, and future
- Understand the value of learning about the past

**future**

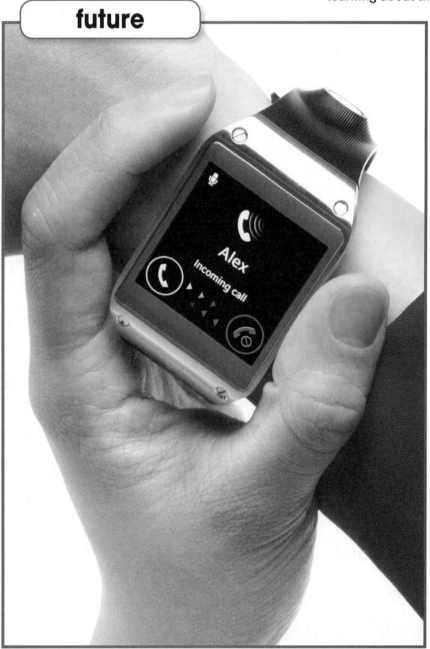

123

# School Days

 **1**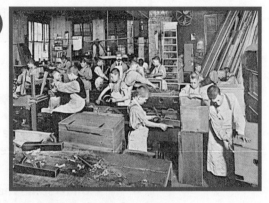

Long ago, many children were unable to attend school. Their families needed them to work.

 **2**

One teacher taught children of all ages reading, writing, and math. Poor schools had a few old books.

 **3**

Today, you have classes for each grade and libraries full of books. Schools will keep changing.

**4**

With two-way video, even when kids are home, they won't miss a thing.

**ThinkSpeakListen**
How many grades does your school have?

# The First Cars

The first car was made in 1769, but cars were not popular until the early 1900s.

In 1908, Henry Ford began making a car called a Model T.

The Model T did not cost much and it worked well.

It changed the way people lived!

**ThinkSpeakListen**
Tell how the Model T looks different from today's cars.

# Education Words

learn

books

teacher

math

**ThinkSpeakListen**

What education word can you add?

# Horses to the Rescue

Tom groaned. He had not seen the hole in the road.

When the front wheel of the car hit it, the car bounced.

It went right into the pond!

"Need help?" Mr. Shay asked.

The horses pulled the car out.

"Give me a horse any day," Mr. Shay said.

On this day, Tom had to agree!

**ThinkSpeakListen**
Tell why Tom had to agree.

# The Story of the White House

## ThinkSpeakListen

Retell important events in the history of the White House.

# The U.S. in Space

In 1961, Alan Shepard became the first American to go into space.

In July 1969, a team of U.S. astronauts landed on the moon.

Today, there are rovers showing us pictures of Mars.

Maybe one day astronauts will land on Mars.

**ThinkSpeakListen**
Talk about what the word "rover" means.

# Using Time Lines

## Chapter 1

Bella and Jay make a time line of a week at school.

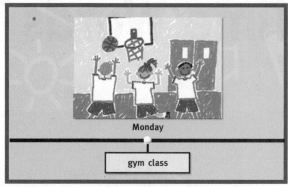

## Chapter 2

Riley and Emma want to make a time line of their school year.

## Chapter 3

This time line shows events that happened in the United States.

## Chapter 4

This time line shows historic buildings.

**ThinkSpeakListen**

What event would begin a time line of your day?

# Time Words

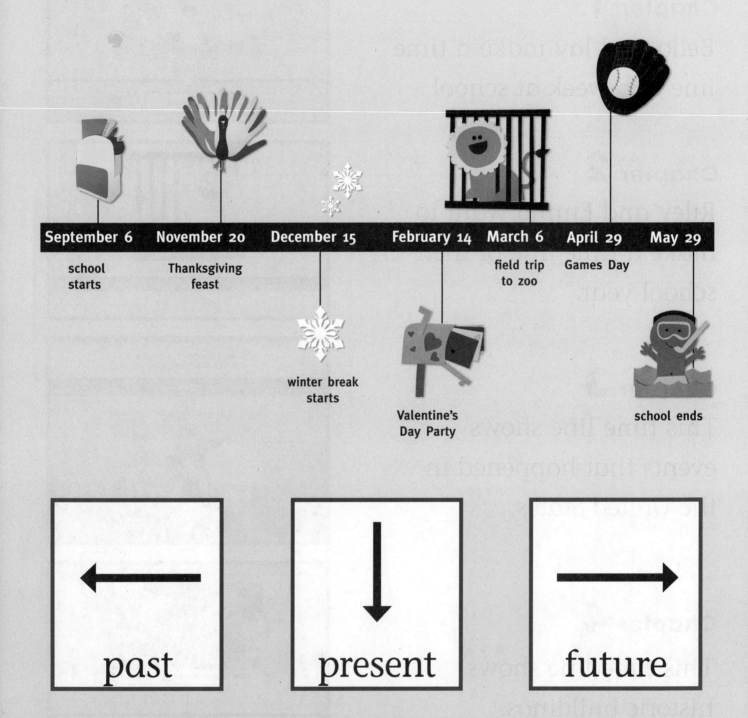

| September 6 | November 20 | December 15 | February 14 | March 6 | April 29 | May 29 |
|---|---|---|---|---|---|---|
| school starts | Thanksgiving feast | | | field trip to zoo | Games Day | |
| | | winter break starts | Valentine's Day Party | | | school ends |

← past

↓ present

→ future

ThinkSpeakListen
Add an event to the time line that happens in the future.

132

# Use Verb Tenses

### present

It is September 6. School **starts** today.

### future

Winter break **will start** in December.

### past

Astronauts **landed** on the moon in 1969.

### future

Maybe one day astronauts **will land** on Mars.

**ThinkSpeakListen**
Tell what you did yesterday.
Tell what you will do tomorrow.

# Using Time Lines

## Chapter 1

A Time Line of a Week at School

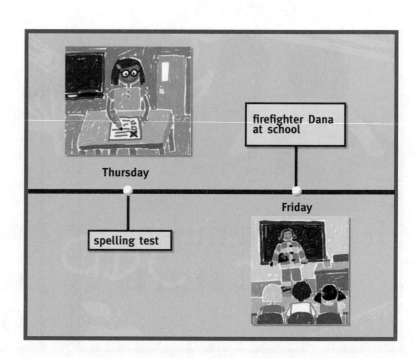

## Chapter 2

A Time Line of the School Year

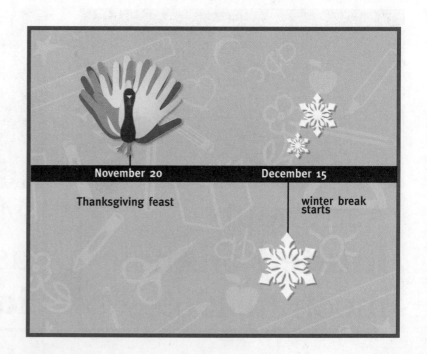

## Chapter 3

A Time Line of the
United States

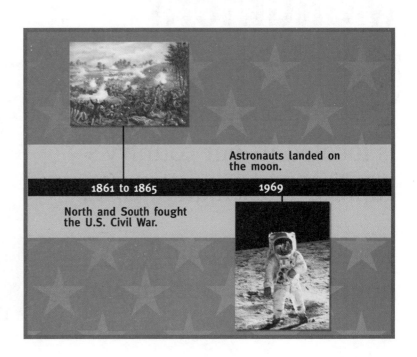

## Chapter 4

A Time Line of Famous
Buildings

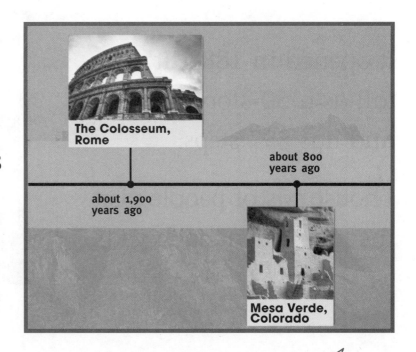

**ThinkSpeakListen**
Tell what each chapter is about.

# The Washington Monument

The Washington Monument is located in our country's capital, Washington, D. C.

The tower was built to honor George Washington.

It opened in 1888. It's as tall as a 50-story building and has 897 steps.

Thousands of people visit the monument each year.

**ThinkSpeakListen**

Which two words use *-ed* to describe something?

# Proper Nouns

## One Name, Three Nouns

the city of Washington, D. C.

President George Washington

the Washington Monument

**ThinkSpeakListen**

Which one of these proper nouns represents a person?

137

# Memorials and Historic Buildings

## Chapter 1

Mount Rushmore is a memorial to honor four **presidents,** or leaders, of the United States.

## Chapter 2

The **Minutemen** fought during the American Revolutionary War. A statue honors these soldiers.

## Chapter 3

The United States Capitol is a historic building in Washington, D. C. The members of **Congress** work here.

## Conclusion

Some memorials honor presidents. Other memorials honor brave **citizens**.

**ThinkSpeakListen**
Tell what each chapter is about.

# Capital Letters

Because **Sacajawea** is a person's name, it begins with a capital letter.

Because our **Capitol** is the only one, it begins with a capital letter.

Because **Lexington** is a place, it begins with a capital letter.

**ThinkSpeakListen**

Talk about why capital letters draw attention to words.

140

# Noun and Verb Agreement

A memorial **honors**.

Visitors **honor**.

A citizen **fights**.

Citizens **fight**.

**ThinkSpeakListen**

What does it tell you when a verb ends in s?

# Observing the
# Sky

My Language Objectives

- Use sky words
- Use comparing words
- Use opposites
- Use nouns
- Use verbs
- Use rhyming words

My Content Objectives

- Build vocabulary related to the sky
- Understand what makes the sky and planets capture our imaginations

## Essential Question

# Why do the sun and moon capture our imagination?

# Why the Sun and the Moon Live in the Sky

**①**

Sun and Moon lived on Earth. One day, Sun asked Sea, "Why don't you visit us?

**②**

"I can't leave my big family," Sea explained. "There isn't enough room in your house."

**③**

So Sun and Moon decided to build a larger house. Sun and Moon invited the Sea and her family.

**④**

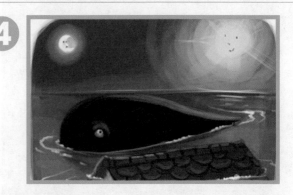

Soon there was four feet of water! When the house was completely covered, Sun and Moon moved up to the sky.

**ThinkSpeakListen**

Do you believe this story? Say why or why not.

144

# A Star Party

"It's dark! Can we start?" Karla asked.

Karla was having a star party with her friends at the farm.

"Yes, let's go," Mom said.

Outside Karla and her friends looked at the sky.

One star was big and bright! Mom told them it was a planet, not a star.

"Let's call it a sky party!" Karla said.

**Think**Speak**Listen**
What mark tells you how excited Karla is at the end of the story?

145

# Sky Words

star

sky

moon

planet

**Think**Speak**Listen**

What can we see from our planet Earth?

# On Mars

A kind of robot called a rover is on Mars now.

It is sending pictures and information back to scientists on Earth.

The rover is a machine, but it can move.

It has "eyes" that are cameras and an arm that can pick up rocks.

Its brain is a computer.

**ThinkSpeakListen**
How is the rover like a car?

# A Walk on the Moon

**3**

**4**

## ThinkSpeakListen

Retell the events of the first moon landing.
First _____. Then _____. Next _____. Last _____.

# The Moon's the North Wind's Cookie

*by Vachel Lindsay*

The Moon's the North
    Wind's cookie.

He bites it, day by day.

The South Wind is a baker.

And bakes a crisp new moon
    that...

*greedy*

North...Wind...eats

    ...again!

**ThinkSpeakListen**
Which word makes the new moon sound tasty?

150

# Night and Day

## Chapter 1

The moon is a round, rocky object that moves around **Earth**.

Many stars fill the sky.

## Chapter 2

The sun is the nearest star to Earth.

Sometimes we see the moon in the sky during the day.

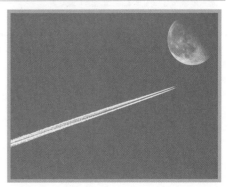

**ThinkSpeakListen**
What subject appears in both chapters?

# Comparing Words

Earth is **big**.

Earth is **bigger** than the moon.

The sun is **far**.

The sun is **farther** than the moon.

**ThinkSpeakListen**

What two letters can make a word mean *more than*?

# Opposites

night

day

big

small

cold

hot

**ThinkSpeakListen**

What is the opposite of *sad*?

# Night and Day

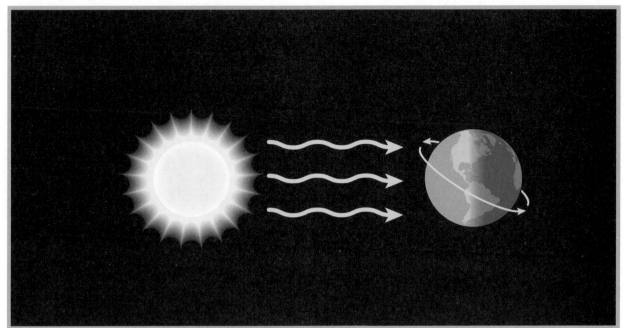

## ThinkSpeakListen

Tell what each chapter is about.

# The Sun

Living creatures on Earth depend on energy from the sun.

Plants use sunlight to make food. Then they grow and give off oxygen.

People and animals breathe the oxygen and eat the plants.

**ThinkSpeakListen**

Tell the steps in how the sun gives us food.
First _____. Next _____. Then _____. Last _____.

# Nouns

star

people

ball

plants

animals

food

**ThinkSpeakListen**

Turn to a partner.
Which of these nouns is a single thing?

# The Wind and the Sun

"I have an idea," said Wind.

"Whichever of us can make the traveler take off his cloak shall be recognized as the strongest."

Harder and harder the wind blew.

*WHOOSH, WHOOSH, WHOOSH!*

The traveler wrapped his cloak tighter across himself.

The sun shone more strongly.
The traveler mopped his brow.

**STRONGER** and **STRONGER**
and **STRONGER** the sun shone.

The traveler opened his cloak.
Then he tore off his cloak and
dropped it on the road.

"I understand now, Sun,"
said Wind.

"The better course is to use
persuasion, not force."

**ThinkSpeakListen**
Retell the story.

# Verbs

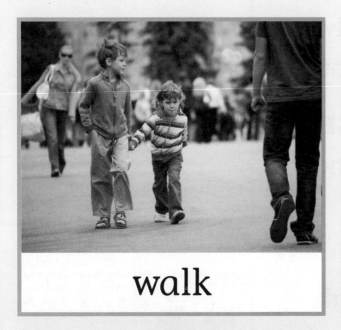

walk

melt

blow

watch

**ThinkSpeakListen**

What does the sun do?

# Rhyming Words

The sun can melt **ice**.

The sun can melt **tar**.

The sun is the hottest thing ever by **far**.

**ThinkSpeakListen**

Tell each other two words that rhyme.

# We Use Goods and Services

goods

goods

# Essential Question

## Why do people trade with each other?

**My Language Objectives**

- Use sequence signal words
- Use categories
- Use noun and verb agreement
- Use punctuation
- Use describing words
- Use prepositions

**My Content Objectives**

- Build vocabulary related to the use of goods and services
- Understand why people trade goods and services with each other

service

service

163

# From Dairy Farm to You

First, the cows must be milked. The milk is pumped into a holding tank.

Next, the milk is pumped into a tank truck.

The truck hauls the milk to a processing plant. The milk goes into bottles.

At last, the milk arrives at the store.

**Think**Speak**Listen**

Retell what happens in the story.
First _____. Then _____. Next _____. Last _____.

164

# Almond Milk

**①**

Some people can't drink dairy milk.

**②**

They drink almond milk instead.

**③**

Making it at home is easy.

First, soak raw almonds in water. Then, pour the water off.

**④**

Blend the nuts with fresh water until the mixture is smooth.

Add vanilla, if you like.

**ThinkSpeakListen**
Which step do you start with? What is the last step?

# Sequence Signal Words

**First,** the cows are milked.

**Next,** the milk goes in the truck.

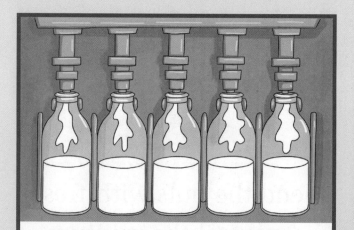

**Then,** the milk is put in bottles.

**Last,** the milk is at the store.

**ThinkSpeakListen**

Which word tells you the steps are over?

# A Farmer's Boy

*Anonymous*

We walked in the lane together;

The sky was covered with stars.

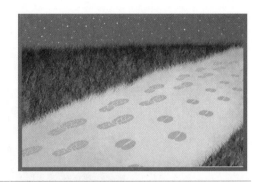

We reached the gate in silence

As I lifted down the bars.

She neither smiled nor thanked me

Because she knew not how

For I was only a Farmer's Boy

And she was a Jersey Cow.

**ThinkSpeakListen**
Does the ending of this poem surprise you? Why?

# The Most Important Service

**1**

**2**

**3**

**4**

Retell the opinions about the most important services.

# Animal Dentists

People aren't the only ones who need dentists.

Animals do, too.

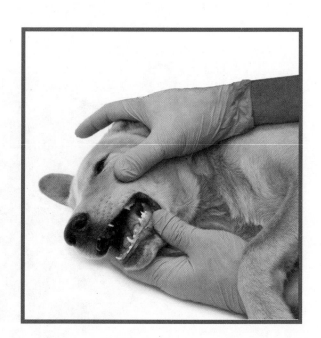

Many animals dislike having their teeth cleaned or fixed.

The dentist uses medicine to make the animal sleep until the job is done.

**ThinkSpeakListen**

Why do you think animals dislike going to the dentist?

# In My Opinion: Goods and Services Are Important

In my opinion, the most important good is food because people cannot live without it.

In my opinion, doctors and nurses provide the most important service because they take care of people.

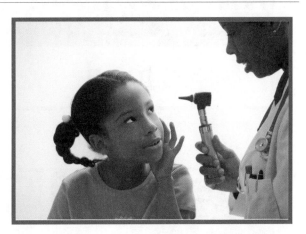

In my opinion, technology goods are important because they make people's lives easier.

**ThinkSpeakListen**
What is another word for *opinion*?

# Categories

### Goods

food

clothes

### Services

nursing

teaching

# Noun and Verb Agreement

They teach.

She teaches.

They farm.

He farms.

**Think Speak Listen**

What does one singer do? What do two singers do together?

173

# In My Opinion: Goods and Services Are Important

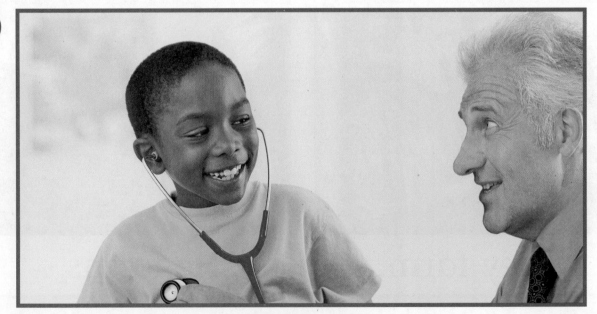

## ThinkSpeakListen

Tell what each part of the story is about.

# Field Trip Funds

Mr. Soto's class was planning a trip to the zoo.

They needed to earn money to pay for the trip.

Some kids wanted to have a book sale at school.

Other kids wanted to walk dogs to make money.

Walking dogs sounded like a job everyone would enjoy.

The class voted, and the dogs won!

**ThinkSpeakListen**
Which would you vote for, the book sale, or walking dogs?

# Punctuation

Stop!

Go!

Sit!

Good!

**ThinkSpeakListen**

Why does an exclamation point get your attention?

177

# The Shoemaker and the Elves

Although the shoemaker worked hard, he could not earn enough money to make a living.

One day all he had left was enough leather to make one pair of shoes.

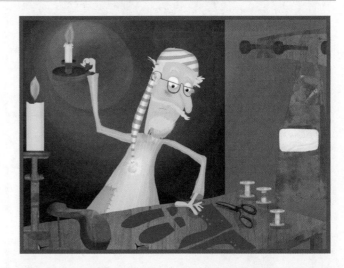

The next morning the shoemaker was amazed to find a perfect pair of shoes on his workbench.

Day after day, the shoemaker woke to find wonderful shoes. The shoemaker said to his wife, "We must find out who is making the shoes!"

Just as the clock struck 12, two tiny elves danced into the room. They hopped up on the bench and began to work.

As they worked, they sang:

*"Stitch, stitch, stitching small and neat. Lovely shoes for lucky feet."*

**ThinkSpeakListen**
Tell what happens in each scene.

# Describing Words

**smoothest** silks

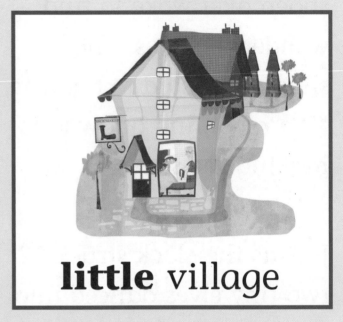

**little** village

**beautiful** shoes

**lucky** feet

## ThinkSpeakListen

Tell another word that describes the shoes the elves made.

# Prepositions

They put clothes **on** the bench.

Then they hid **in** the cupboard.

They put **on** the clothes.

They danced **in** their new clothes.

**Think**Speak**Listen**

Say two things you see around you.
Tell where they are.

181

# Exploring Sound and Light

**My Language Objectives**

- Use cause and effect signal words
- Use sound words
- Use sentence patterns
- Use opposites
- Use compound nouns

**My Content Objectives**

- Build vocabulary related to sound and light
- Understand the ways in which sound and light affect our lives

## Essential Question

How would our lives be different without sound and light?

# Sounds I Love!

**1**

The fire trucks shriek and clang,

Construction workers boom and bang.

**2**

The city is the place for me.

Because I love the sounds, you see.

**3**

Horses neigh and owls say hoo,

I wake each morning to COCK-A-DOODLE-DO!

**4**

The country is the place for me.

Because I love the sounds, you see!

**ThinkSpeakListen**

What sound do cars stuck in traffic make? What sound do chickens make?

# Dogs Help the Deaf

Some sounds, like a beeping car, warn you to watch out.

Some people may not hear those sounds, because they are deaf.

A furry friend called a "hearing dog" can help them.

The dog learns to turn and look at something it hears.

Then its owner turns to look, too.

Hearing dogs are helpful pals!

**ThinkSpeakListen**
What does the mark at the end of the last line tell you?

# Cause and Effect Signal Words

Some people do not hear those sounds **because** they are deaf.

**Because** they are deaf, they get a "hearing dog."

**Because** they have a "hearing dog," they can cross the street.

**ThinkSpeakListen**

Tell what causes someone to get a "hearing dog."
What is the effect of having a "hearing dog" if you are deaf?

# I Know All the Sounds That the Animals Make

*by Jack Prelutsky*

I know all the sounds that
the animals make,

and make them all day from
the moment I wake,

I roar like a mouse and I purr
like a moose,

I hoot like a duck and I moo
like a goose.

I croak like a cow and
I bark like a bee,

no wonder the animals marvel
at me.

**ThinkSpeakListen**

What funny trick runs through this poem?

187

# Shadow Puppets

1

**ThinkSpeakListen**

Tell how shadow puppets work.

# Rainbow

Hard rain falls,
    I'm stuck inside.

I'd rather get my bike
    and ride.

The sun peeks out and
    says to rain,

"It's time for me to shine
    again."

The streets and puddles
    start to dry,

And then a rainbow
    paints the sky.

**Think** Speak **Listen**

Tell which words are rhyming words.

# I Hear with My Ears

I have two ears—they're
quite a sight!
They fit my head so nice
and tight.

Some sounds are very, *very* LOUD:

Thunder crashing in a cloud.

Other sounds are soft and
sweet:

Slippers swishing on my feet.

The sounds that cheer me
when I'm blue?

Baby's babble, giggle, coo.

**Think**Speak**Listen**

Tell about sounds you hear on the street.
Tell about sounds you hear in the woods.

# Sound Words

crashing

swishing

babble

giggle

**Think**Speak**Listen**

Tell another sound a baby makes.

# Sentence Patterns

My ears **are** there to help me hear.

**Are** my ears there to help me hear?

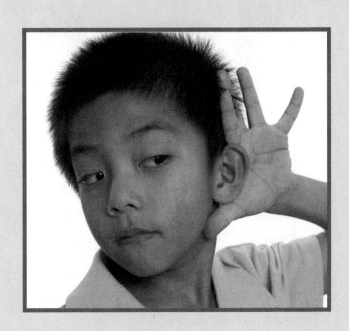

The job they do **is** very clear.

**Is** the job they do very clear?

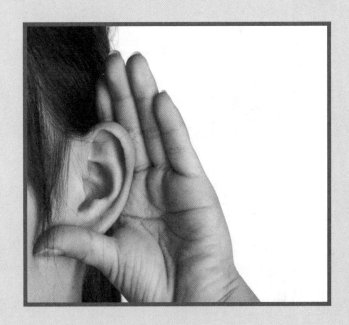

**ThinkSpeakListen**
What happens to the verb to make the sentence into a question?

193

# I Hear with My Ears

**5**

**6**

**7**

**8**

# Day or Night?

What is the difference between day and night?

Near the North Pole, the answer is not so clear. One day each fall, the sun sets.

Then it doesn't rise again for about eight weeks.

The opposite happens each spring. One day, the sun rises.

It doesn't set for eleven weeks!

**ThinkSpeakListen**
What does the mark at the end of the first sentence tell you?

# Opposites

night

day

dark

light

rises

sets

**Think**Speak**Listen**

What is the opposite of *cold*?

# The Light Around Us

**Chapter 1**

Seeing Objects

**Chapter 2**

How Light Moves

# Chapter 3
## Exploring Light

## Conclusion
Light is important in everyday life.

**ThinkSpeakListen**
Tell what each chapter is about.

# Compound Nouns

sunlight

flashlight

headlights

**ThinkSpeakListen**

Tell when you would use a flashlight.

# Sentence Patterns

Some objects allow light to pass through.

**Do** some objects allow light to pass through?

You can see yourself in the mirror.

**Can** you see yourself in the mirror?

**Think**Speak**Listen**

What had to be done to turn each sentence into a question?

# Common Core State Standards

## CA CCSS Reading Standards for Literature

| RL.1.1 | Ask and answer questions about key details in a text. |
|---|---|
| RL.1.2 | Retell stories, including key details, and demonstrate understanding of their central message or lesson. |
| RL.1.3 | Describe characters, settings, and major events in a story, using key details. |
| RL.1.4 | Identify words and phrases in stories or poems that suggest feelings or appeal to the senses. **(See grade 1 Language standards 4–6 for additional expectations.) CA** |
| RL.1.5 | Explain major differences between books that tell stories and books that give information, drawing on a wide reading of a range of text types. |
| RL.1.6 | Identify who is telling the story at various points in a text. |
| RL.1.7 | Use illustrations and details in a story to describe its characters, setting, or events. |
| RL.1.9 | Compare and contrast the adventures and experiences of characters in stories. |
| RL.1.10 | 10. With prompting and support, read prose and poetry of appropriate complexity for grade 1.<br>**a. Activate prior knowledge related to the information and events in a text. CA**<br>**b. Confirm predictions about what will happen next in a text. CA** |

## CA CCSS Reading Standards for Informational Text

| RI.1.1 | Ask and answer questions about key details in a text. |
|---|---|
| RI.1.2 | Identify the main topic and retell key details of a text. |
| RI.1.3 | Describe the connection between two individuals, events, ideas, or pieces of information in a text. |
| RI.1.4 | Ask and answer questions to help determine or clarify the meaning of words and phrases in a text. **(See grade 1 Language standards 4–6 for additional expectations.) CA** |
| RI.1.5 | Know and use various text **structures (e.g., sequence) and text** features (e.g., headings, tables of contents, glossaries, electronic menus, icons) to locate key facts or information in a text. **CA** |
| RI.1.6 | Distinguish between information provided by pictures or other illustrations and information provided by the words in a text. |
| RI.1.7 | Use the illustrations and details in a text to describe its key ideas. |
| RI.1.8 | Identify the reasons an author gives to support points in a text. |
| RI.1.9 | Identify basic similarities in and differences between two texts on the same topic (e.g., in illustrations, descriptions, or procedures). |
| RI.1.10 | With prompting and support, read informational texts appropriately complex for grade 1.<br>**a. Activate prior knowledge related to the information and events in a text. CA**<br>**b. Confirm predictions about what will happen next in a text. CA** |

## CA CCSS Reading Standards for Foundational Skills

| RF.1.1 | Demonstrate understanding of the organization and basic features of print.<br>a. Recognize the distinguishing features of a sentence (e.g., first word, capitalization, ending punctuation). |
|---|---|
| RF.1.2 | Demonstrate understanding of spoken words, syllables, and sounds (phonemes).<br>a. Distinguish long from short vowel sounds in spoken single-syllable words.<br>b. Orally produce single-syllable words by blending sounds (phonemes), including consonant blends.<br>c. Isolate and pronounce initial, medial vowel, and final sounds (phonemes) in spoken single-syllable words.<br>d. Segment spoken single-syllable words into their complete sequence of individual sounds (phonemes). |
| RF.1.3 | Know and apply grade-level phonics and word analysis skills in decoding words **both in isolation and in text. CA**<br>a. Know the spelling-sound correspondences for common consonant digraphs.<br>b. Decode regularly spelled one-syllable words.<br>c. Know final -e and common vowel team conventions for representing long vowel sounds.<br>d. Use knowledge that every syllable must have a vowel sound to determine the number of syllables in a printed word.<br>e. Decode two-syllable words following basic patterns by breaking the words into syllables.<br>f. Read words with inflectional endings.<br>g. Recognize and read grade-appropriate irregularly spelled words. |

## CA CCSS Writing Standards

| W.1.1 | Write opinion pieces in which they introduce the topic or name the book they are writing about, state an opinion, supply a reason for the opinion, and provide some sense of closure. |
|---|---|
| W.1.2 | Write informative/explanatory texts in which they name a topic, supply some facts about the topic, and provide some sense of closure. |
| W.1.3 | Write narratives in which they recount two or more appropriately sequenced events, include some details regarding what happened, use temporal words to signal event order, and provide some sense of closure. |
| W.1.5 | With guidance and support from adults, focus on a topic, respond to questions and suggestions from peers, and add details to strengthen writing as needed. |
| W.1.6 | With guidance and support from adults, use a variety of digital tools to produce and publish writing, including in collaboration with peers. |
| W.1.7 | Participate in shared research and writing projects (e.g., explore a number of "how-to" books on a given topic and use them to write a sequence of instructions). |
| W.1.8 | With guidance and support from adults, recall information from experiences or gather information from provided sources to answer a question. |

## CA CCSS Speaking and Listening Standards

| SL.1.1 | Participate in collaborative conversations with diverse partners about *grade 1 topics and texts* with peers and adults in small and larger groups.<br>a. Follow agreed-upon rules for discussions (e.g., listening to others with care, speaking one at a time about the topics and texts under discussion).<br>b. Build on others' talk in conversations by responding to the comments of others through multiple exchanges.<br>c. Ask questions to clear up any confusion about the topics and texts under discussion. |
|---|---|
| SL.1.2 | Ask and answer questions about key details in a text read aloud or information presented orally or through other media.<br>**a. Give, restate, and follow simple two-step directions. CA** |
| SL.1.3 | Ask and answer questions about what a speaker says in order to gather additional information or clarify something that is not understood. |
| SL.1.4 | Describe people, places, things, and events with relevant details, expressing ideas and feelings clearly.<br>**a. Memorize and recite poems, rhymes, and songs with expression. CA** |
| SL.1.5 | Add drawings or other visual displays to descriptions when appropriate to clarify ideas, thoughts, and feelings. |
| SL.1.6 | Produce complete sentences when appropriate to task and situation. (See grade 1 Language standards 1 and 3 for specific expectations.) |

# CA CCSS Language Standards

| | |
|---|---|
| L.1.1 | Demonstrate command of the conventions of standard English grammar and usage when writing or speaking.<br>a. Print all upper- and lowercase letters.<br>b. Use common, proper, and possessive nouns.<br>c. Use singular and plural nouns with matching verbs in basic sentences (e.g., *He hops; We hop*).<br>d. Use personal (**subject, object**), possessive, and indefinite pronouns (e.g., *I, me, my; they, them, their; anyone, everything*). **CA**<br>e. Use verbs to convey a sense of past, present, and future (e.g., *Yesterday I walked home; Today I walk home; Tomorrow I will walk home*).<br>f. Use frequently occurring adjectives.<br>g. Use frequently occurring conjunctions (e.g., *and, but, or, so, because*).<br>h. Use determiners (e.g., articles, demonstratives).<br>i. Use frequently occurring prepositions (e.g., *during, beyond, toward*).<br>j. Produce and expand complete simple and compound declarative, interrogative, imperative, and exclamatory sentences in response to prompts. |
| L.1.2 | 2. Demonstrate command of the conventions of standard English capitalization, punctuation, and spelling when writing.<br>a. Capitalize dates and names of people.<br>b. Use end punctuation for sentences.<br>c. Use commas in dates and to separate single words in a series.<br>d. Use conventional spelling for words with common spelling patterns and for frequently occurring irregular words.<br>e. Spell untaught words phonetically, drawing on phonemic awareness and spelling conventions. |
| L.1.4 | Determine or clarify the meaning of unknown and multiple-meaning words and phrases based on *grade 1 reading and content,* choosing flexibly from an array of strategies.<br>a. Use sentence-level context as a clue to the meaning of a word or phrase.<br>b. Use frequently occurring affixes as a clue to the meaning of a word.<br>c. Identify frequently occurring root words (e.g., *look*) and their inflectional forms (e.g., *looks, looked, looking*). |
| L.1.5 | With guidance and support from adults, demonstrate understanding of word relationships and nuances in word meanings.<br>a. Sort words into categories (e.g., colors, clothing) to gain a sense of the concepts the categories represent.<br>b. Define words by category and by one or more key attributes (e.g., a *duck* is a bird that swims; a *tiger* is a large cat with stripes).<br>c. Identify real-life connections between words and their use (e.g., note places at home that are *cozy*).<br>d. Distinguish shades of meaning among verbs differing in manner (e.g., *look, peek, glance, stare, glare, scowl*) and adjectives differing in intensity (e.g., *large, gigantic*) by defining or choosing them or by acting out the meanings. |
| L.1.6 | Use words and phrases acquired through conversations, reading and being read to, and responding to texts, including using frequently occurring conjunctions to signal simple relationships (e.g., *because*). |

# California English Language Development Standards

## CA ELD Part I: Interacting in Meaningful Ways

| | |
|---|---|
| ELD.PI.1.1 | Exchanging information and ideas with others through oral collaborative conversations on a range of social and academic topics |
| ELD.PI.1.2 | Interacting with others in written English in various communicative forms (print, communicative technology, and multimedia) |
| ELD.PI.1.3 | Offering and supporting opinions and negotiating with others in communicative exchanges |
| ELD.PI.1.4 | Adapting language choices to various contexts (based on task, purpose, audience, and text type) |
| ELD.PI.1.5 | Listening actively to spoken English in a range of social and academic contexts |
| ELD.PI.1.6 | Reading closely literary and informational texts and viewing multimedia to determine how meaning is conveyed explicitly and implicitly through language |
| ELD.PI.1.7 | Evaluating how well writers and speakers use language to support ideas and opinions with details or reasons depending on modality, text type, purpose, audience, topic, and content area |
| ELD.PI.1.8 | Analyzing how writers and speakers use vocabulary and other language resources for specific purposes (to explain, persuade, entertain, etc.) depending on modality, text type, purpose, audience, topic, and content area |
| ELD.PI.1.9 | Expressing information and ideas in formal oral presentations on academic topics |
| ELD.PI.1.10 | Writing literary and informational texts to present, describe, and explain ideas and information, using appropriate technology |
| ELD.PI.1.11 | Supporting own opinions and evaluating others' opinions in speaking and writing |
| ELD.PI.1.12 | Selecting and applying varied and precise vocabulary and language structures to effectively convey ideas |

## CA ELD Part II: Learning About How English Works

| | |
|---|---|
| ELD.PII.1.1 | Understanding text structure |
| ELD.PII.1.2 | Understanding cohesion |
| ELD.PII.1.3 | Using verbs and verb phrases |
| ELD.PII.1.4 | Using nouns and noun phrases |
| ELD.PII.1.5 | Modifying to add details |
| ELD.PII.1.6 | Connecting ideas |
| ELD.PII.1.7 | Condensing ideas |

## CA ELD Part III: Using Foundational Literacy Skills

| | |
|---|---|
| ELD.PIII.1.1 | See Appendix A [in *Foundational Literacy Skills for English Learners*] for information on teaching reading foundational skills to English learners of various profiles based on age, native language, native language writing system, schooling experience, and literacy experience and proficiency. Some considerations are:<br>• Native language and literacy (e.g., phoneme awareness or print concept skills in native language) should be assessed for potential transference to English language and literacy.<br>• Similarities between native language and English should be highlighted (e.g., phonemes or letters that are the same in both languages).<br>• Differences between native language and English should be highlighted (e.g., some phonemes in English may not exist in the student's native language; native language syntax may be different from English syntax). |

# Benchmark ADVANCE

# Texts for English Language Development

Credits
Editor: Joanne Tangorra
Creative Director: Laurie Berger
Art Director: Jieting Chen
Production: Kosta Triantafillis
Director of Photography: Doug Schneider
Photo Assistant: Jackie Friedman

Photo credits: Cover A: © Sheng Li / Reuters; Table of Contents: ©KidStock/Blend Images; Page 8C, 17A, 17C, 18A, 18B, 19A, 19B, 20C, 20D, 20E, 21A, 21B, 21C: Granger, NYC; Page 9A: © Corbis; Page 14A: © Tony Freeman / PhotoEdit; Page 14B: © Anna Peisl/Corbis; Page 16A: © Photos 12 / Alamy; Page 17B: Library of Congress; Page 56C: © Rolf Nussbaumer Photography / Alamy; Page 82-83: © Sheng Li / Reuters; Page 84B, 101B: ZSB/WENN.com/Newscom; Page 84C, 101C: Xinhua/Photoshot; Page 84D, 101D: © GAUTIER Stephane/SAGAPHOTO.COM / Alamy; Page 85B: © CORBIS; Page 94A, 95A: © Kim Kulish/Corbis; Page 94C: © Agencja Fotograficzna Caro / Alamy; Page 113A: Filipe Frazao / Shutterstock.com; Page 123: © Oleksiy Maksymenko Photography / Alamy; Page 124b: Universal Images Group/Newscom; Page 124c: AP Photo/David Duprey; Page 125b: Omikron; Page 125c: Three Lions; Page 128b: © North Wind Picture Archives / Alamy; Page 129a: © CORBIS; Page 130a: Everett Collection; Page 130c, 133e: NASA/Science Source; Page 136b: PhotosJC / Shutterstock.com; Page 138b: Granger, NYC; Page 139b, 140a: © Franz-Marc Frei/Corbis; Page 169b: © ZUMA Press, Inc / Alamy; Page 169c: © dmac / Alamy; Page 185b: John Birdsall/Rex/REX USA; Page 186b: Lee Busby/Mirrorpix/Newscom

Art credits: Page 10: Sernur Isik; Page 13: Elizabet Vukovic; Page 25: Sernur Isik; Page 27: Tiziana Longo; Page 32: Tiziana Longo; Page 65: Marcin Piwowarski; Page 70: Marcin Piwowarski; Page 76: Bill Greenhead; Page 77: Becka Moore; Page 80: Louise Pigott; Page 87: Tony Trimmer; Page 90: Tony Trimmer; Page 100: Becka Moore; Page 105: Aleksandar Zolotic; Page 106-107: Bill Greenhead; Page 110: Elizabet Vukovic; Page 116: Jillian Altmeyer; Page 127: Giusi Capizzi; Page 145: Alexander Wilson; Page 150: Louise Pigott; Page 166: Richard Watson; Page 167: Giusi Capizzi; Page 176: Alexander Wilson

ISBN: 978-1-5021-6643-2 (hardcover)
ISBN: BE2774 (paperback)